True Crime:

Deadly Serial Killers And Gruesome Murder Stories From The Last 100 Years

Hank Gatsby

Table of Content

Introduction
Charles Frederick Albright
    Victims
    Verdict
Edmund Emil Kemper III
    Victims
    Verdict
Hamilton Howard "Albert" Fish
    Victims
    Verdict
Richard Trenton Chase
    Victims
    Verdict
Carl Panzram
    Crimes
    Conviction & Execution
Conclusion

Introduction

A serial killer is defined as being a person who murders three or more people. The murders usually give the killer an abnormal amount of gratification, either psychological or physical – often both. The murders can take place over more than a month and include significant breaks between them which are called 'cooling off periods'; however, this is not always the case.

There are more than two hundred *convicted* serial killers in the United States alone. Imagine the number in the entire world! Some of the most horrifying acts of violence are committed by serial killers though not all serial killers are especially violent. Serial killers are almost always looking for their next victim. They kill over and over again and are never fully satisfied by their bloody deeds. Their twisted motivations and techniques cause police to label these people as the most frightening criminals in history.

Each homicide case that law enforcement officers across America respond to on a daily basis is tragic. However, there are few cases more stomach-churning and more difficult to understand than serial murder. The topic of serial murder occupies a unique niche within the community of criminal justice. Serial murder cases attract a lot of attention from the media, mental health experts as well as the general public.

Anyone who enjoys crime drama on television will be familiar with Criminal Minds; the BAU out of Quantico, a branch of the FBI that only gets involved when asked by the local law enforcement? Well, the one thing the show doesn't tell us is that the BAU is actually 4 different units under the 'banner' titled the National Center for the Analysis of Violent Crime (NCAVC). While Morgan, Hotchner, Rossi, et al fly around the country in their private jet following the cases they are asked to join in on the investigation ... the real BAU groups specializing in certain crimes and working on solving those cases. In the case of serial murders the local law enforcement might work with two or three different units; BAU-2 (Crimes against adults), BAU-3 (Crimes against children) or ViCAP (Violent Criminal Apprehension Program). BAU-1 concentrates exclusively on terrorist threats and crimes.

Serial murder isn't a new phenomenon and it's not uniquely American either. However, the obsession that people have regarding serial killers and their atrocities seem to have been fed by Hollywood's productions. The story lines are created in order to heighten the interest of audiences rather than to accurately portray serial murder. Focusing on the atrocities inflicted on victims by 'deranged' killers, the public is captivated by the criminals and their crimes which only leads to more confusion to the true dynamics of serial murder.

Serial murders are relatively rare events with less than one percent of all murders committed in any year or location being the result of a serial killer. Ever since 'Jack the Ripper' in the late 1880s and the series of unsolved prostitute murders in London people have been fascinated with serial killers. Let's indulge ourselves, shall we?

Please be advised that the contents of this book may be graphic and is not suitable for some audiences.

Charles Frederick Albright

Known as the Texas Eyeball Killer, Albright was a natural born sociopath and killer. He murdered and raped a total of three victims between December 13, 1990 and March 18, 1991. He was apprehended four days after the discovery of his third victim. He was arrested and charged with the three murders and his trial began December 13, 1991 – one year after the discovery of his first victim.

Victims

- December 13, 1990 – Mary Lou Pratt was Albright's first victim. She was a well known prostitute in the Oak Cliff neighborhood of Dallas, TX. Reports were filed that a half-nude woman had been found lying in the road. The children who found Mary Lou's body reported that she had almost looked like a manikin laying in the road. Mary Lou Pratt had been shot in the back of the head with a 44 caliber handgun. Her shirt had been pulled up around her neck to expose her breasts; this would become one of Albright's trademarks. When an autopsy was performed it was found that Mary Lou's eyeballs had been removed. It had been done with a precision that suggested a surgeon may have performed the excision and murder. There were no leads and no forensic evidence in this case so it soon went cold.

- February 10, 1991 – Susan Peterson, another prostitute, was discovered dumped in South Dallas outside of the city limits. Her shirt was pulled up around her neck revealing her breasts just like the previous victim had been displayed. Susan was shot three times rather than just once; through the top of the head, in the left breast and in the back of the head. The medical examiner found that this victim had also had her eyeballs surgically removed. There was apparently a connection between Susan Peterson and Mary Lou Pratt since Susan revealed to police that she knew who had killed Mary Lou. Unfortunately, she did not give police the name of the killer.

- March 18, 1991 – Shirley Williams was a part-time prostitute and was found naked, laying in a street near a school in the same vicinity of the previous two murders. This time it was obvious that the killer was becoming more vicious and careless. Officers found a used condom near the body and, when she was taken for autopsy, a piece of metal was found embedded in her eye socket. It was determined to be from an exacto-type knife which was used to remove the eyeballs. Shirley had facial bruises, a broken nose and had been shot through the top of her head as well as in the face.

Verdict

The only solid evidence the prosecution had against Albright were hairs found on the third victim, Shirley Williams, which forensically matched Charles Albright. Despite most of the case being circumstantial, prosecutors were able to achieve a conviction. On December 18,1991 he was found guilty of one count of murder and sentenced to life in prison.

Edmund Emil Kemper III

Also known as Big Ed, The Co-Ed Butcher and The Co-Ed Killer, Kemper is a sociopath, serial killer and necrophile. He was active in California in the early 1970s but he started his criminal career in the early to mid 1960s. As a 15 year old boy he admitted to shooting his grandmother just to see what it felt like. He then shot his grandfather and hid the body, later telling the police that he had shot his grandfather to keep the man from finding out that his wife had been murdered.

Kemper was committed to the Atascadero State Hospital in 1964 after admitting to the killing of his grandparents but he showed sociopathic traits much earlier in his childhood. From a young age he had tortured and killed animals, sometimes eating the remains raw. He had acted out bizarre sexual rituals with his sister's dolls and admitted that the only way he could kiss a teacher he had a crush on was to kill her. Kemper's mother did not help the situation and probably contributed to his sociopathic tendencies with her constant berating and humiliation. Her reasoning was because she was afraid he would molest his sisters or harm them in some fashion. After serving less than 5 years, Kemper had managed to convince the doctors at the State Hospital that he was reformed which lead to his release from that institution. His juvenile records were sealed with his release back into society in 1969.

From May 1972 to April 1973 Edmond Kemper went on a murder spree that started out with six female students and didn't end until he murdered his mother and her best friend. Somehow he had managed to stay one step ahead of authorities during this time. It is thought that he had befriended many Santa Cruz County police officers and regularly hung out with them at their favored watering hole, The Jury Room. Apparently none of these friends had any suspicions about Kemper and discussed the case with him rather freely.

Victims

- August 27, 1964 – Maude Matilda Hughey Kemper. Edmund Kemper's grandmother was working on her latest children's book at the kitchen table when she and 15 year old Kemper began arguing. She was shot in the head. Edmund Emil Kemper, the grandfather, returned from grocery shopping and was fatally shot in the driveway before his body was hidden nearby.

- May 7, 1972 – Mary Ann Pesce and Anita Luchessa, two 18 year olds were hitchhiking. They were Fresno State students Kemper picked up on the pretext of taking them to Stanford University. He drove for about an hour before finding a secluded wooded area near Alameda. There he smothered and stabbed Pesce to death before fatally stabbing Luchessa as well. Reports state that Kemper loaded both bodies into his trunk and returned to his apartment. Once there he took pornographic pictures of the naked corpses before dismembering them. He orally raped both women's heads then put all the body parts into plastic bags, dumping the bags in an abandoned area near Loma Prieta Mountain. Both heads were thrown into a ravine.

- September 14, 1972 – Aiko Koo was a 15 year old who was hitchhiking to her dance class after she missed the bus. Kemper picked her up and held her at gunpoint as he drove to a secluded section of road where he strangled her to death before raping her corpse.

- January 7, 1973 – Cindy Schall, a 19 year old Cabrillo College was picked up by

Kemper. He drove her to a secluded wooded area and shot her with a 22 caliber pistol. Putting her body into his truck he returned to his mother's house and kept her body in his room overnight. As a 'joke' he buried Cindy's severed in his mother's garden facing up toward his mother's bedroom window. He later remarked that his mother wanted people to look up to her. Kemper then dismembered Cindy's body and discarded the remains in a ravine.

- February 5, 1973 – Rosalind Thorpe (24 yo) and Alice Liu (23 yo) encountered Kemper after he had left his mother's home after an argument. Kemper stated to police that Rosalind had entered his car first which reassured Alice and caused her to enter as well. After leaving the university Kemper fatally shot both women with a 22 caliber pistol. Wrapping both bodies in blankets he placed them in the backseat of his car. It is reported that he sexually abused their corpses and then dismembered the bodies the next morning. The remains were discarded at Eden Canyon near San Francisco where they were discovered about a week later.

- April 20, 1973 – Clarnell Strandberg Kemper and Sally Hallett. On Good Friday Kemper fell asleep while waiting for her to return from a party. He waited until she had gone to bed before entering her room to see her reading. He stated to police that she had said, 'I suppose you want to sit up all night and talk now?' to which he replied, 'No, good night.' before beating her to death with a claw hammer. Once his mother was dead Kemper decapitated her, orally raped the severed head and then used it as a dart board. He also removed her vocal cords and attempted to put them down the garbage disposal but the machine could not break down the tough tissue and ejected it back into the sink. Kemper then called Sally Hallett, his mother's best friend, to come over to the house. He strangled Hallett after her arrival. Once his mother's friend was dead Kemper left the scene of his final crime.

After killing his mother and her best friend Kemper drove to Pueblo, CO. When he had not heard any news on the radio about his last two murders he called the police. The police did not believe him and told him to call back at a later time. Several hours later he again called and asked to speak to an officer known to him personally. He confessed to the murders of his mother and Sally Hallett but did not mention the six female students until after his arrest. He waited in his car until the police arrived to arrest him and take him into custody.

Verdict

Edmund Kemper plead 'not guilty' by reason of insanity at his trial. He was found guilty in November 1973, after the prosecution's three psychologists declared Kemper sane. He had asked for the death penalty but California had suspended capital punishment at that time. Instead he received life in prison without the possibility of parole. After a short observational period in the California Medical Facility Stat Prison at Vacaville he was finally transferred to the maximum security Folsom Prison where he remains to this day.

Hamilton Howard "Albert" Fish

Also known as the Gray Man, the Werewolf of Wysteria, the Brooklyn Vampire, the Moon Maniac, and The Boogey Man, Albert Fish was a child rapist, cannibal and serial killer. He had boasted that he 'had children in every state' and that he had victimized more than 100 children. It is not known whether he was referring to rapes or cannibalization or even if it was the truth. At the time of his arrest Fish had confessed to three murders though he was suspected in at least five more murders during his lifetime. He was finally arrested, tried and convicted for the kidnapping and murder of Grace Budd.

Not even Ted Bundy, David Berkowitz, Jeffery Dahmer or any of the well-known serial killers can hold a candle to the depravity and fiendishness of the seemingly kind and harmless Albert Fish. With a quiet facade and silver hair and mustache he looked like every child's favorite uncle or grandfather. However, behind that serene exterior lurked a hideous monster. He preyed on the young and innocent and admitted to molesting more than 400 children in a span of about 20 years. This man lived a life of unparalleled perversity.

Victims

Known Victims

- July 14, 1924 – Francis McDonnell, eight years old, was reported missing by his parents. An organized search of the Port Richmond neighborhood of Staten Island soon found his body. He had been hung in a tree near his home. He had been sexually assaulted and then strangled with his suspenders. He had also suffered lacerations to his legs and abdomen and the left thigh had been almost entirely stripped of flesh. Witnesses had told police that the boy had been seen with an elderly man with a gray hair and drooping gray mustache; Francis' mother had admitted seeing a similar man earlier in the day. It was this description that gave Fish the moniker of 'The Gray Man'. The McDonnell murder had remained unsolved until the murder of Grace Budd when Albert Fish finally confessed to that murder as well. Fish had stated that he had planned to castrate the boy as well but had fled when he thought he heard someone approaching the area.

- February 11, 1927 – Billy Beaton (3 yo) and Billy Gaffney (4 yo). The two boys disappeared when Billy Beaton's older brother left the two younger boys alone playing in the apartment hallway in Brooklyn. Billy Beaton's body was later found on the roof of that apartment building. When asked what had happened to the boy, the older Beaton boy said that 'the bogeyman' had taken him. Gaffney's body was never recovered. Fish later admitted in a letter written to his attorney that he had tortured, mutilated, dismembered and ate Billy Gaffney except for the head, hands, arms and legs beneath the knee which were put in potato sacks and weighted with stones. It is thought that those body parts were dumped in the river.

- May 25, 1928 – Grace Budd was not Fish's intended victim at this time. Her older brother, Edward, had advertised for a job in the local newspaper which Fish had seen and visited the Budd household to offer the 18-year-old a job. He had planned on tying Edward up, mutilating him and leaving the young man to bleed to death. However, when he met the Budd family his plans changed. He offered to hire both Edward and his friend Willie to work on his farm but that he would send for them in a few days. Fish failed to show up to pick up the boys but sent a telegram to apologize and set a later date. When he arrived he made up a story about a niece's birthday party and convinced Grace's parents to allow him to accompany her to the party that evening. Grace never returned home. The Budd's later received a letter purported to be from Fish detailing the gruesome nature of their daughter's demise. The letter lead the police to Fish and was part of the evidence used against him during his trial.

Suspected Victims

- October 3, 1926 – Emma Richardson, age 5.
- Unknown month, 1927 – Yetta Abramowitz, age 12.
- July 13, 1930 – Emil Aalling, age 4.
- May 2, 1931 – Robin Jane Liu, age 6.
- February 15, 1932 – Mary Ellen O'Conner, age 16.
- December 15, 1932 – Benjamin Collins, age 17.

Verdict

The trial against Albert Fish for the murder of Grace Budd began on March 11, 1935 in White Plains, NY. The trial lasted for 10 days and Fish pleaded guilty by reason of insanity. He stated that God was telling him to kill children. Several psychiatrists testified for the prosecution that Fish was a 'psychiatric phenomenon'. His sexual fetishes included sadism, masochism, cunnilingus, anilingus, fellatio, flagellation, exhibitionism, voyeurism, piquerism, cannibalism, coprophagia, urophilia, pedophilia and infibulation. Nowhere in legal or medical records from the early 1900s to the present time has any serial killer exhibited so many abnormalities.

Albert Fish was convicted of one count of first degree murder and sentenced to be executed. He arrived at Sing Sing prison in March of 1935 and was executed on January 16, 1936. He entered the execution chamber at 11:06pm, strapped into the electric chair and was pronounced dead three minutes later. After the conclusion of the execution James Dempsey, Fish's lawyer, told reporters that he was in possession of his client's final statement but he refused to ever show it to anyone.

Richard Trenton Chase

Also known as The Vampire of Sacramento, Chase committed six murders in just one month in Sacramento, CA. He was called the Vampire of Sacramento because he drank the blood of his victims and ate their internal organs.

By the time he was a teenager he was already displaying two of the three common traits amongst serial killers; killing and mutilating animals as well as fire-starting. It is only suspected that he was also a bed-wetter but it is likely since he already exhibited the other two traits of the sociopathic triad.

Chase was born in 1950 and was raised very strictly by his parents, his father often beat him. He became an alcoholic in his teens and started killing and mutilating animals. While he had girlfriends while in high school he was unable to maintain a steady relationship. It was documented by a psychiatrist that the inability to maintain and erection or be aroused around females was caused by either repressed rage or mental illness. After this diagnosis there was no record that Chase received further treatment. It was later determined that he had an aversion to conventional sex and was only able to become aroused and climax when performing violent or disturbed acts such as killing animals and necrophilia.

In 1975, Chase was committed to a mental institution. He had been taken to a the emergency room for blood poisoning. Chase had told doctors that he had injected himself with rabbit's blood. He managed to escape from that hospital but was soon apprehended and sent to an institution for the criminally insane. After a battery of treatments Chase was deemed no longer a danger to society despite a schizophrenic diagnosis, and released into his parent's custody in 1976. Soon after his release his mother weaned him off of the medication to control his schizophrenia.

When he was released his parents arranged an apartment for him. He began to capture, torture and drink the blood of rabbits, dogs and cats, occasionally killing and eating his neighbor's pets. At about this time he developed a fascination with firearms and purchased several handguns and began practicing obsessively.

Chase began his murder spree on December 29, 1977. This was just two days after he fired a 22 caliber handgun into the home of a Sacramento woman. The slug was found in her kitchen but since no one was harmed no charges were filed.

Victims

- December 29, 1977 – Ambrose Griffin, a 51 year old engineer and father of two. Chase killed Griffin in a drive by shooting that was apparently a 'warm-up' for the killings he planned to commit. A neighbor's 22 caliber rifle was confiscated and tested but was determined not to be the murder weapon in the Griffin case. However, the bullet taken from Griffin's body was determined to come from the same gun as had fired the bullet into the kitchen of the Sacramento woman two days earlier.

- January 23, 1978 – Teresa Wallin, a 22 year old pregnant woman was surprised in her home by Chase as she returned from taking out the garbage. Chase reportedly told police that he found unlocked doors as an invitation to enter. Wallin was shot three times, once in the hand and twice in the head. He then dragged her into the bedroom where he raped her corpse while stabbing her several times with a large kitchen knife. Wallin's body had been cut open and several organs removed and evidence showed that Chase drained a large amount of blood to bathe in before cutting off a nipple and drinking her blood from an empty yogurt container. Before Chase left he went into the yard, collected some dog feces and returned to the bedroom to stuff into the victim's mouth.

- January 27, 1978 – This is the date of Chase's final murder which qualifies as a mass murder. The victims were: Evelyn Miroth (38yo), David Ferreira (22 months), Jason Miroth (6yo) and Dan Meredith (a neighbor of unknown age). Meredith was the first to fall when the man confronted Chase in the front hallway, he was shot point blank in the head with a 22 caliber handgun. Jason ran into his mother's bedroom where he was shot twice in the head. As Chase was following Jason, David was also shot in the head. Evelyn Miroth was shot once in the head when Chase entered the bathroom. He then dragged the body onto the bed where he simultaneously sodomized it and drank blood from a series of slices at the back of the neck. Once finished he stabbed the victim's corpse several times which caused blood to pool within the abdominal cavity. Chase drained the pooled blood and drank it all. Retrieving David's corpse, he took it to the bathroom, split open the child's skull and consumed some of the brain matter. Fleeing the scene when a knock on the door interrupted him, Chase took David's body home with him. Once there he cut off the toddler's penis and used it as a straw to drink the blood from the body. Several internal organs were consumed and 'smoothies' made of others before the corpse was finally disposed of at a nearby church.

Verdict

Five days after the mass murder Chase was determined to be the perpetrator of the Wallin and Miroth murders. Detectives went to Chase's apartment and asked to speak with him, when Chase refused they waited down a hallway. Chase left his apartment carrying a bloodstained box, his parka and shoes were also bloodstained. Inside the box were shreds of bloody wallpaper and the 22 caliber pistol he had used to commit his murders. When he was searched, Dan Meredith's wallet was found.

In 1979 Chase was put on trial for six counts of first degree murder in which the defense tried to have the charges reduced to second degree murder based on Chase's history of mental illness and the fact that the murders were not premeditated. On May 8 a jury found Chase guilty of all six counts of first degree murder. The defense requested a clemency hearing where a judge determined that Chase was not legally insane. Chase was sentenced to die in the gas chamber. While waiting to die Chase was feared by the other inmates who tried to convince him to commit suicide since they were too fearful to get close enough to him to murder him themselves.

While in prison Chase granted a series of interviews with Robert Ressler where he indicated a fear of Nazis and UFOs. He claimed that he had killed his victims in order to keep himself alive since he believed that Nazi UFOs were trying to turn his blood into powder. He requested access to a radar gun with which he thought he could apprehend the Nazi UFOs. Before Ressler left the last interview Chase handed over a large amount of macaroni and cheese which he had been hoarding in his pants pocket. He stated that the guards were trying to poison him because they were in league with the Nazis.

On December 26, 1980 during a bed check by guards Chase was found dead in his bed. An autopsy determined that Chase committed suicide with an overdose of the antidepressants he'd been prescribed by the prison doctor. He had saved the pills for a few weeks.

Carl Panzram

Unlike many other serial killers, Carl Panzram was not given a catchy nom de guerre by either investigators or the media of the time. However, he did use several aliases; Carl Baldwin, Jack Allen and Jefferson Baldwin while in Oregon; Jeff Davis in Idaho; Jefferson Davis in California; Jeff Rhodes in Montana; and John King or John O'Leary in New York.

Born in 1891 to a poor farming family in Minnesota, his father abandoned the family when he was about 8 years old. Panzram was soon committed to a reform school called Red Wing for several burglaries. It could be said that Red Wing made Panzram who he became. Throughout his time at Red Wing he was punished with beatings and rapes which led him to decide that since the world was so terrible he was going to go through it and wreak as much havoc as he could.

After graduating from Red Wing young Panzram spent years homeless and sleeping on freight trains. During a ride in a boxcar he was gang raped by transients which left him a sadder, sicker but wiser boy. 1915 found him traveling through Idaho, California and other states along the Columbia River.

Panzram admitted to committing 21 murders and more than 1000 rapes of young men and boys. He served time in jails and prisons in California, Texas, Idaho, Montana, Oregon, Connecticut, New York's Sing Sing, Clinton Correctional Facility in New York, Washington DC and Leavenworth in Kansas.

Crimes

On June 1, 1915, Panzram was in Astoria, OR where he burglarized a house and was soon arrested when caught attempting to sell some of the stolen items. He was sentenced to seven years in Oregon State Penitentiary in Salem. Harry Minto was the warden who believed in harsh treatments of inmates under his supervision. Panzram was disciplined several times while he was incarcerated which included 60 days in solitary confinement. Minto was murdered by fellow inmate Otto Hooker when Hooker escaped with the help of Panzram. On September 18, 1917 he escaped from prison. He was involved in two shootouts before he was returned to the prison. However on may 12, 1918 he escaped again and this time he was able to avoid capture and hopped a freight train and headed east. He changed his name to John O'Leary and shaved off his moustache, never returning to the northwest.

In August 1920 Panzram burglarized future President Taft's New Haven, CT home where he stole a large amount of jewelry and bonds as well as Taft's Colt M1911 45 caliber handgun which were then used in his murders.

Panzram committed his first murders in late 1920. Sailors were lured away from bars in New York to a yacht he had purchased with the bounty from his various burglaries. After getting the men drunk he raped them and then shot them. The bodies were dumped into the river. This killing spree was only stopped when his vessel ran aground near Atlantic City, NJ where his last two potential victims managed to escape from the floundering yacht.

Luanda, Angola was purportedly his next destination according to his biography. He claims to have raped and murdered a young boy and hiring a row boat so that he could kill the rowers and throw their bodies to the crocodile. He claimed there were six rowers in all. Before leaving Africa he claimed to have raped and murdered another boy which became his 'favorite kill' because the boy had begged and pleaded for his life before being strangled to death.

Returning to America Panzram claimed that he had shot a man for attempting to rob hm and that he had raped and killed two small boys; one being beaten to death with a rock on July 18,1922 and the other being strangled later in the year in New Haven, CT.

Panzram's last arrest occurred in 1928 where he claimed to have committed a murder while breaking and entering homes between Baltimore and Washington DC as well as a murder in Philadelphia, PA. Three of the last five killings attributed to Carl Panzram are confirmed.

Conviction & Execution

In 1929 a judge sentenced Panzram a 25 year sentence to be served at Leavenworth Federal Penitentiary for his extensive criminal record. Records indicate that he told the warden upon arrival that he would kill the first man that bothered him. On June 20, 1929 Robert Wamke, foreman of the prison laundry, was killed by Panzram. Wamke was beaten to death with an iron bar. After that murder he was convicted and sentenced to death by hanging. He refused to appeal and threatened human rights groups that attempted to appeal on his behalf.

Panzram was executed on September 5, 1930. When the executioner put the noose around his neck he supposedly spat in the executioner's face and declared that he wished all mankind had one neck so that he could choke it. The question of if there were any last words seemed to amuse Panzram who replied that he wished the man would hurry up because he could kill ten men while the man was 'fooling around'.

Carl Panzram has been labeled a misanthrope and history's most sadistic serial killer. He is also brutally honest. In his biography he states, "For all these things, I am not the least bit sorry." and "I hate the whole damned human race, including myself." His biography was written while he awaited execution in Leavenworth, the manuscript was entrusted to Henry Lesser who was a guard on death row. Lesser pressed for it to be published for forty years after Panzram's execution and it was finally released as *Killer: A Journal of A Murder* in 1970. A 1996 movie of similar name was based on Panzram's last years with James Woods portraying Panzram. The original manuscript was donated for archival material to the San Diego State University in 1980.

Conclusion

Well-known American serial killers bring Ted Bundy, Jeffery Dahmer, John Wayne Gacy, Dennis Rader (BTK Killer) and many others to mind. However, deeper investigation show that while they are cunning and charming – they are far from the perpetrators of the most gruesome and grisly crimes in history.

The five men written about in this book are some of the most depraved men to walk the earth in the last century. They committed some of the most heinous, stomach-churning crimes to date. We may never know the true number of victims they murdered, mutilated and desecrated or the number of lives they destroyed on their criminal pathways.

Despite studies or the profiling done by the FBI's special task forces it remains as Wednesday Adams said in the Adam's Family movie when asked where her Halloween costume was. "I'm a homicidal maniac. They look just like everyone else."

Your Free bonus

Eye Contact Training

Introduction

Hello!

I want to thank you and congratulate you for downloading "Eye Contact Training".

This book was written for everyone out there that is suffering from anxiety and poor eye contact. As you all know eyes are the windows to the soul and if you cannot maintain eye contact with the opposite gender or with anyone really, it will be really hard for that person to trust you and your true intentions.

You deserve a lot of value and this book was written to serve you and help you to better your life. I promise you that if you follow these steps in this book you will be on your way to maintaining perfect eye contact with everyone you meet and you will have less social anxiety. Learning to improve your eye contact and your communication skills will greatly improve your quality of life. You will learn that your business life, social life, and your connections with other people will improve drastically as a result of better eye contact and body language.

Why Eye Contact is So Important

Eye contact is so important because you have to remember that the eyes are the windows to the soul. What that means is that you can lie but your facial expressions and your eyes will give it away. When you lie your body gives off a distinct facial expression as if you are trying to hide something and if you can maintain eye contact you can detect the things that people are saying when they aren't saying anything.

Eye contact is also something that almost every high status person has. Its something that every CEO and important person in the world can maintain. This is why eye contact is so important. When you can maintain eye contact people will look at you like you are important. They want to see if you can handle the tension of maintaining eye contact and if you have experience in high tension situations

You might even say that eye contact is crucial for maintaining attraction with women. Think about it this way, lets say a woman looks at you and you immediately look away. You are signaling to that woman that you are being submissive to her, woman don't like submissive men because they are submissive by nature. They want dominant men that can handle themselves in any situation that comes across them.

If you are a man that can maintain eye contact when a beautiful woman looks at you, then you are signaling to her that you are dominant, you are not afraid, and it is conveying a high social status to her. Basically you are being attractive as you can possibly be by having good eye contact.

Maintaining eye contact is demonstrating your power over yourself and your emotions. The woman will feel that power and become overwhelmed by sexual attraction. When she looks into your eyes she doesn't just notice your eyes, she notices everything that comes with good eye contact. The subtext that you can't read on the surface but she is thinking in the back of her mind.

Do yourself a favor and commit to this training so that you can become the best version of yourself. If you can't maintain eye contact with a beautiful woman, then how in the hell are you going to bring her on your bed.

So lets begin.

What is the difference between high status eye contact and low status eye contact?

What high status eye contact means is that you are looking at your world in a relaxed and confident manner. What this means is that you will be looking around when you want slowly and surely. The world is your playground all these people are living in your world, you are not sharing this world with anybody, they are merely living in your world. This means that your eye contact will not be affected by any external stimulus. You will feel calm and relaxed when you are looking at a woman or anybody.

You need to be become grounded when you are looking at a woman, for example you notice a beautiful woman standing across the street and you turn to catch a look at her. When she turns around and catches you looking at her, you will not look away because you feel like you have been caught. No you will not be ashamed you will keep looking into her eyes and you will look away only when you want to look away.

But keep into mind social norms. You do not have to be staring into the eyes of every person that walks down the street. You can hold your eye contact for a couple of seconds and look away if you want. You do not have to be staring at someone for more than 1 minute, this isn't high status behavior.

You can either be high status or low status just by your patterns of eye contact. Do not over do eye contact because you will be remembered as that creepy guy who stares at people all the time. Maintain eye contact with people naturally, and trust your what your instincts are telling you. They will be correct.

I will introduce to you the first rule of eye contact.

When you are talking to someone you must maintain eye contact 85% of the time and look into one eye. When you look into one eye the effect is more powerful because both of your eyes are fixated onto one thing. The other 15% of the time you will look away either at the distance behind them to organize your thoughts.

When somebody else Is talking to you, you will only maintain eye contact with them about 60% of the time. When they are talking to you, look into their eyes and slowly look away. Remember you will make them fight for your attention and eye contact because it is valuable and you are high status.

Always remember that a high status person moves slowly so make sure when you turn your head and your eye contact it is slow and not anxious.

Eye Contact Techniques

Now you have a little background with high status eye contact and what it means to have high status eye contact.

We will get into different eye contact techniques that you can use in your life to raise your status higher in everyday situations when you talk to people.

The first technique that I want you to learn is to keep your head still and your body still when you are communicating with someone. The person that is the least nervous and moves less when they are talking is perceived as the higher status person. Put this into action and you will notice the difference in the way woman look at you, and you will see the difference in their eyes.

The second technique is related to the opposite sex. When you are communicating with woman you will notice that sometimes their eyes seem a little wider than usual and they seem bigger and more excited. This means that the woman usually has an interest in you that's why their eyes are lighting up. When you see this in the different interactions throughout the day with woman, what you want to do to amplify this attraction to this next level is to basically squint with your eyes.

I want you to think of George Clooney, if you don't know who he is then google him. You need to practice squinting your eyes when you talk and maintain dialogue with people. One of the most important things is your facial features and how much control you have over your face.

I want you to practice talking to yourself in a mirror everyday. The reason for this is because I want you to notice how you look when you talk and if you really think that you are being attractive. With a mirror you can constantly judge and evaluate yourself and your facial expressions to see if they are attractive or not.

The mirror is one of mankind's greatest inventions because you can literally see yourself. The first thing to practice in the mirror is your squint. When you squint a little bit you look a lot more attractive and woman will notice it your facial expression.

When you are squinting, what this does is sub communicating to that woman that you don't want to take the full picture in. This will send a message to the girl, I'm not sure about you. When you send that message with your body language, this will make the girls think to themselves, why isn't he sure about me?

When the girls are thinking this to themselves, they will subconsciously try to get you to like them so they can validate themselves. Woman like being validated and do not like feeling unsure of their worth. By understanding this one little principle, you can use your facial expressions to dictate the flow of the conversation and the meaning behind the words.

Another trick that I have mentioned previously are the pupils. If you are unsure whether or not a girl likes you, then all you need to do is to look at her pupils. If they are dilated and bigger than they usually are for a normal person. You will be able to tell, because her eyes will light up in a different way than if you were talking to your friends. Than you will know that she likes what she is hearing and seeing in front of her.

Eye Contact Training Exercises

Sorry for keeping you wait this long. Now you will learn the ultimate eye contact training techniques to take your life to the next level. When you do this exercises consistently over time you will notice that your behavior will start to change. You will be having flawless eye contact, and this will lead you to develop deeper relationships with people at work. You will also notice a lot more female interaction going to your favor. Stick with the training this will be the beginning of a new life.

Lets Begin!

1. Eye contact Attention training techniques

This exercise is that when you are talking to someone you are going to look into their eyes, pick one. When you are talking you will maintain eye contact 90% of the time and look directly into one pupil and the other 10% of the time you will look at the background behind them in order to collect your thoughts. Sometimes you can even through a squint in there.

When they are talking to you, however you will only maintain eye contact 60% of the time and make them fight for your attention. You will only look at them if they say something of substance or something that interests you. If you become disinterested it is okay to look away. You can still listen to them, but you can direct your eye contact somewhere else. They will have your ears, but they won't have your full attention.

2. Slow relaxed confident movements

People that are slow and take their time to do things show a high status behavior. They are not nervous, but they are always slow composed and calm during any interaction and when they go about their daily lives.

3. Having a Still head

When you have a still head and do not move your head around, people will look at you with at a higher status. When you do not care to move your head around to look at things only your eyes, this demonstrates high status behavior.

These three techniques will have you feeling like a more high status and more dominant person.

Anxiety Training Techniques

1. Single Focus technique

This is the first of many tension training techniques that you will learn that will help you improve your eye contact. What you will need is a television or a computer screen and a tiny object. You will place the tiny object on top of the television or computer screen and play a movie on silent. What you will proceed to do is focus on the tiny object for sixty seconds. What this does is to train your discipline and focus muscles to only focus on the tiny object while the movie is playing in the background. If you feel your eyes drawn to the movie its okay, just focus your attention back to the tiny object on top of the computer or television. You will do this exercise three times. Take a break after 60 seconds and repeat 2 more times.

2. Cold Showers

While this exercise is not directly related to using your eyes it will help in maintaining eye contact from another person. What you will need to do is whenever you take a shower from now on it will be freezing cold. This will help you to learn how to breathe during uncomfortable situations you will learn how to breathe deeply. When you continue to take cold showers you will notice that the water will not feel as cold as the first time. This is the same thing you will be doing for your eye contact, every time you practice making good eye contact you will notice that it feels less and less uncomfortable. It might even feel easy after a few weeks.

3. Deliberate eye contact

This exercise may be a little difficult, I recommend doing this with caution. What you will do is to stare into the eyes of a person 1 time every day and get caught. What this means is that you will stare at that person and when he or she turns to look at you, you will continue to look into their eyes for a good 3 seconds before turning away. This will train you to maintain eye contact under the most tension. If you do this 1 time every day either when you are walking, taking the train, or buying groceries you will notice that eye contact will become easy for you.

These exercises are meant to be done everyday or else they will not work. You cannot expect to be great at anything if you do not practice every day with consistency.

Facts about eye contact

When you make eye contact with another person, this produces a powerful subconscious effect on that other person. This will increase rapport and likeability between the two people.

People reduce eye contact when they talk about something shameful or embarrassing when they are sad or depressed, or when they are accessing internal dialogue and emotions.

People that can maintain good eye contact are associated as being more dominant and powerful. They are also considered more warm and personable. They are more attractive to the opposite sex. Even when applying for jobs they are considered more qualified, skilled, and valuable. In social situations they are considered more trustworthy, confident, and emotionally stable.

There are too many benefits of having good eye contact that it would be detrimental to your future success if you did not master this skill.

Why Eye Contact is Important

1.   Our eyes were
   made to connect

The whites in our eyes made it very easy for other people to see exactly what we are looking at and very easily notice when our focus changes. So that means that if you think the other person does not know where you are looking at, you are dead wrong. The eyes were made in order to communicate better with others.

2.   The eyes reveal
   your inner thoughts and feelings

Whether or not you feel like telling the truth, your facial expressions and your eyes will always give you away. You can read someone by just looking closely and observing their eyes and facial expressions.

Principles for making effective Eye Contact

When you start making more eye contact with another person they will usually follow suit and take your lead. Many people are afraid to make more eye contact with another person because, they are scared they won't reciprocate. The truth of the matter is that many people are looking for permission to make eye contact. What this means is that if you want to make greater eye contact with another person do so. The other person will follow suit and make the same amount of eye contact with you.

Do not be creepy. When you want to initiate eye contact with another person it is important that the eye contact is mutually agreed on. So if you try to initiate eye contact with another person and you have tried several times but it is not reciprocated then move on to the next person.

Eye contact for specific Scenarios

Business and sales

When you are giving criticism or feedback to an employee, when you sit directly across to them face to face, this will make the conversation seem very hostile and interrogating. What you should do is sit from a 45 degree angle from your employee, this will make the conversation seem more natural and easy. You will be able to shift your eye contact comfortably between your employee and the paper work in front of you.

Making Sales

When you are trying to make a sale, making eye contact is crucial to building trust and rapport with the other person. If you try to selling someone something without looking at them in eye then you are in the wrong business. If you do that, you will communicate dishonesty and shame, in your product or whatever you are selling. When you look at them in the eye you will build trust and rapport very quickly. Another tip is when you are maintaining eye contact, make note when they initiate it with you. This will usually signal that you've said something interesting that you want them expand upon. They are giving you the clues and hints as to what they want to know more about and how you can close the sale.

Making a Pitch

When you are making a pitch to a group of people, don't just look at your boss or the VP in charge. You need to look at everybody that is in the room for your pitch to be effective or else it will just look like you are sucking up in front of your boss.

A job Interview

During a job interview, it is crucial that you maintain good eye contact with the other person. In a study done, employers were much more likely to hire those who maintained a normal amount of eye contact with the hiring manager than those who continually looked away.

Conclusion

Now is the time to take all of this knowledge with you and continue to practice your eye contact throughout your day. You have learned about all the benefits of eye contact in your business life, your personal life, and your love life. There is so much potential in having good eye contact.

If you commit to practicing and doing these exercises for one month, I can guarantee you, that your life will benefit so much from these exercises. You will notice more attention from women. You will start commanding respect from your peers and they will start to look at you for decisions and people will even start doing things for you.

Now is the time to take everything you have learned and apply it to your daily activities to transform your life.

Thank you and good luck!

www.ingramcontent.com/pod-product-compliance
Lightning Source LLC
Chambersburg PA
CBHW070928180526
45168CB00005B/2197